Shadow Box

First published in the United Kingdom in 2023 by
Shearsman Books
P.O. Box 4239
Swindon
SN3 9FN

Shearsman Books Ltd Registered Office
30–31 St. James Place, Mangotsfield, Bristol BS16 9JB
(this address not for correspondence)

www.shearsman.com

ISBN 978-1-84861-848-0

Shadow Box

Gerrie Fellows

Shearsman Books

CONTENTS

The Curiosities of Dr Hunter / 7

Without Image / 11

Kaitaka / 12

Waka Huia / 13

Wooden Box with Brass-hinged Lid / 14

Altar, Sandstone / 15

Mirror / 16

Nest / 17

Object: Carved Stone Ball / 18

Calculus / 19

Cast / 20

Three Hands / 21

Gold Struck Coin with Shadow / 22

After-image / 23

Optical / 24

Log of Intermittent Tracings / 25

Mars Drill Bit / 26

Engine / 27

Vitrine / 28

Notes and Acknowledgements / 32

THE CURIOSITIES OF DR HUNTER

Dr Hunter's cabinet of marvels
polished to a high gloss
frames the body parts of beauties
a nymph

dry-pinned
the sheen of a carapace
the startling sash of brilliant wings
fixed under mirroring glass

Neptune beetle   made up of parts
head and thorax of a true Scarab
staked to paper
a recipe for a fake

or an invention
for the naturally curious to unravel

as Lady St Aubyn's gift
of Cornish ores
(the raw core of tin mines)
was an invitation to know the ground

the mineral heart of his collection
six hundred jaspers   agates
translucent as insect wings
lucid amber   traders' gems

quartz in a chert concretion
one of Pocock's petrified melons
delicious but inedible
case of mistaken identity

and identification
was the name of the game
God's perfect arrangements
thrown into doubt

by the fossil sequence
unearthed
from coal measures or limestone
Cuvier's proof of extinction

Corals   insects   shells
the wealth
of Dr Fothergill's collection
a purchase on nature's profusion

the *Endeavour's* prize   flower
and artifice of southern oceans
the materia of a living culture
or relics for an age of wonder?

for his antiquarium   a case
of the long-gone swaddled dead
(grave good was to come of it
and did)

all manner of curiosities
even Linnaeus

original of the collecting mind
preserved here   a bronze medal

beside the image of fortune
a mother with her sun king
embraced in a silver roundel
bulbed as a pregnant womb

The core of the matter
in the doctor's mind
(before the Rembrandts
the Hogarth engravings)

manuscripts   incunabula
historical medical treatises
books as hooks to hang his thinking on
anatomical samples

wet specimens and dry bones
diseased and intricate as coral
the bony eminence
of a skull deformed

the anatomy of the human
gravid uterus
ravaged yet no grave goods
for his cabinet of curiosities

(though the book's a cabinet too)

a woman   nine months pregnant
newly dead   cut open in secret
revealed in cross section
on the page's two dimensions

a natural object   unidentified
(habitat London   Camberwell Beauty?)
her death   an instruction
for science   and the safety of royals

Jars   drawers   trays of glass
wood sheened to high gloss
to polish off the stain of rumour
a shimmer

as if the body of knowledge
were exposed   flayed to muscle

the man of natural curiosities
(up-and-coming anatomist
obstetrician to royalty)
makes his own entrance

in history   (reputation intact)
a man of science   winging it
among butterflies and body parts
and his own death mask

WITHOUT IMAGE

Having seen   half a lifetime ago
how can I put out of mind

the void in which a human being
was   and was not object

chiselled with the bones of birds
inked with ash of resinous trees

bartered for muskets and metal
in an age of traded objects

displaced   displayed

the unsolved clues of moko
dishonoured by sight

he who was not   and is subject

the dead   sacred
released at last into place

KAITAKA

Rectangular cloak in a single weave
South Island, New Zealand (18th century)

flax, double-twined
ornamented with clusters of feathers
a patterned edge   encased
as if without weight against weather

there is a question of distance
a question of orientation
a border   the direction of feathers
meanings hidden or brought forward

how to understand what is seen
as a map of the past
or as a map with the tracks of birds

groundweave of tussock and flax tuft
bird calls knotted into it   kiwi feathers
          orange (as of small fires)
          night-sky blue of pukeko

a knowledge passed down in the body
          flighty   or earthbound

a question the weaver answers
netting sky and windblown earth

WAKA HUIA

Treasure box with replica huia feathers
North Island, New Zealand (19th century)

Bird canoe   precious vessel
carved to hang aloof from roofbeams

observed from an angle of shadow
faces furrowed fiercely downward   prows
to protect white-tipped tail-feathers
wrapped in totara bark and flax

Observed in the forest's reflection
          (lightwaves diffracted)
the huia's tail-feathers
were a sheen of iridescence

observed from logged forests
vanished   left only the colour of pigments

Fake feathers cannot replicate
the wattlebird's shimmering absence

Waka huia, with shadow
its faces prows to protect a ghost
an island unvoiced
a bird canoe   riding light waves

WOODEN BOX WITH BRASS-HINGED LID

made by the carpenter on the Resolution
for 14-year-old midshipman Alexander Hood

to box compass and spirit level
instruments of the elemental
souvenirs, keepsakes from home
unfolding
      to brassy cold

        a silence laced with hawsers
        billow of sails   waves not streets
        not grain   not songbirds
        gulls' cries   islands of ice

        imago   disproved
by chart and crossing   by his captain's rigour
by the accuracy of chronometers
lines imagined on the paper of maps
                    unsightable

        Terra Australis Incognita

        ghost land   seabird's feather

ALTAR, SANDSTONE

dedicated by Marcus Cocceius Firmus
centurion of the Second Legion Augusta

to Silvanus
who in the beginning was wild
a spirit of branches   birch spindles
the wooded maze
out of which only a god may bring us

arrow in flight
through a puzzle of leaves
all that rustles in the unkent
smoke and burnt timber of native smelters
silence   inhabited by the wild
a portal through which the other slips into us

Silvanus
guardian of woods and fields
god of enclosures   god of turfed bank and ditch
god of boundaries
do not let me be lost
do not erase me

MIRROR

tin bronze alloy (fragments), Leckie Broch
Iron Age Chronology, Roman

Double-layered
polished finely then scratched in polishing

Who scoured smoke and shadow
for a self newly reflected   (no longer body)

who searched for an inverted image
mirage in a polished surface

metal alloy, with face   (not yet fragmented)

who now is brought to light
framed in the soul's smashed windows?

Who brings to light   in fragments
of reflection   the object's altered purposes

glass display case   with face, leaning in
a decoy from another order   observer

reassembling from smoke and mirrors
figments   of who
                who sees   and is seen?

NEST

Taxonomy: meadow pipit (Anthus pratensis)
field study, Trossachs

A perfected structure
of wiry grass
dry, snow-bleached stalks
lined with hair silk
straw-coloured softness
pale as a pipit's feathering
streamers of song
      spirals down to speckled eggs
      and harboured mimicry

The nature of nest
cupped shelter lapped under wing
eggs cached in nature's hide-and-seek
how could it be without hazard?
The cross-hatched network
nestles a clutch of flutterers
or a gauky hustler

Out of eyeshot
the moorland's nestless flier
      Displayed behind glass
      no bird   cuckoo or pipit
      no egg or nestling

      g/host nest   with absence

OBJECT: CARVED STONE BALL

403.6 grams. Locality: Aberdeenshire
3200–2500 BCE

Handheld   a weighted sphere
deeply grooved to fit a fingering
the whole hand takes part in

a plaything for the mind
come to us from the past   iron-dark
speckle of biotite in granular stone
worked by Neolithic hands
in a tooled, ancient trade

The mind asks for meaning
gets a curve ball, carved   ancestrally wielded
an object willed
                    but not into the unknown

Unknown is only where we find ourselves
enquirers desiring to recognise
a symbol of power
    an artefact of ceremonial
        a device for speech   memory   story

for guesswork   our best guess
for an object blessed with guesses

        turning   as if in the dark

    We are in the dark
    the object shines in the light
                glitters with Scottish earth

CALCULUS

Bladder Stone, calcium oxalate,
uric acid, phosphates

A bodily concretion
budded from the blood
mineral salts   particles charged
to a distilled essence of self

a sediment
that muddies the body's waters
to a banded whirlpool   concentrated
maddens in its padded cage
cached, unendurable   pain unhatched

Hatched is what the observer sees
a coddled oddity
lassoed by an eighteenth century hoop
the wreckage of lithotomy
or a fractal mascerated to a calcite dross

Like a shadow in the bladder
the distant augury of ultrasound
the far-flung shrapnel of a big bang

the body's concentricities spun out of orbit
yet of the body still

The self   absent
the body-stone becomes the object

CAST

of the left hand of Frederyk Chopin
Medium: bronze

Gold-knuckled in metallic skin
inhuman   scattering light

the stilled dimension
of bones, flexed tendons
the hypermobile
immobilised to a single piece

his dead hand   plastercast
in transition from being to artefact
cast from the body
to sombre bass notes

keys his living hand had spanned
string and hammers
sounding the heart's velocities

The ear, too, has a hammer
as had the craftsman who shaped
the shell of wood and air
in which the music resonates

from which all the living notes
rise up   as if weightless
yet bearing the weight of grief and love

cast to the air where sound plays
on the small bones of the ear

THREE HANDS

made in the pattern shop of Yarrow and Co.
for the Erskine hospital (1914–18)

from a wood
rooted in water-logged ditches
handfuls of chlorophyll and air
dried to a static curve

fingers lined with dark inlays
thumbs jointed   like parts of a rifle
disassembled in living hands

all those delicate, mobile junctures
blood vessels, nerve pathways
splintered bone
the old life   a finished thing

Between each mutilated man
and the longed-for, generous, tactile world

a gap   (skin he must lean his face to)

as if the mind could trigger his lost fingers
(brain bereft, nerves of the stump aflame)

the ghost of his hand   a minding

GOLD STRUCK COIN WITH SHADOW

Ryal, Edinburgh mint, 1555
7.58 grams

In profile, facing left   a woman's face
as if she could not have been a child   promised
not yet a bride   an imagined queen
absent from her own kingdom

Who is she   *Mary, by the grace of God*

an image with tilted head, crossed pearls
her fair copy fixed
her outline backed by lion rampant
on a coin minted from Scottish gold

or the fake   *4.56 grams,*
                                           maker unknown
a half-weighted alloy core struck in perfect detail
MARIA. DEI. G. SCOTOR. REGINA
head just a tilt out
crown beadless   angling east

on a surface dulled by base metal to a stain of peat
tempered   resistant   indurate
true metal of the kingdom she was a stranger in

but of Mary herself   all images are false

AFTER-IMAGE

(Photogram for Emily Dix 1904–1972
pioneer palaeobotanist)

In morning vapour   a trace
on the window pane of a single dragonfly
or was it a shadow that alighted here
as if among seed fern and horsetail

her findings
from the black fuel of the coalfields –
a tweed-skirted field geologist
whose inventive mind crossed the boundaries
of the Upper Carboniferous

On display
findings that survived wartime bombing
Neuropteris attenuata, Lepidodendron ophiurus

but not range charts, research notes
her thoughts
that burned bright as fern fronds in coal

No note of the frontal leucotomy
that cut through a mind
high-flying through seed fern and horsetail
Neuropteris schlehani, Annularia stellata

The image on the glass
(diffuse as a foot print in snowmelt)
unfossilised, mutable imprint
Emily Dix among the nine floral zones
of the Upper Carboniferous

OPTICAL

Compound binocular microscope
brass, steel, lead, glass (19th century)

Observer of the invisible
Galileo's telescope   inverted
from a dark field of stars to insect life
Hooke's honeycomb cells of cork

Seen through the eyepiece
animalcula, capillaries, red blood cells
the small rain of the microscopic world

All this has happened   but not in this direction
it's light that brings the object to the eye
a bright field of cholera bacilli
or the nucleus of a cell

In the body tube
a mind-bending dance fans out
        upended   magnified
                a virtual image of what's to come

        a single trembling molecule   centred
in the eye's perceptual lens

like light from the sun
or the point sources of stars   an image
from the far field of a distant slide
enters
                the brain's
                                decoding somersault

LOG OF INTERMITTENT TRACINGS

Processor unit with gold-plated heatsink
(Electrocardiology Research Unit)

intel (R) PENTIUM (R) PRO
plain logo on the heatsink's flat gold
over the invisibly intricate pattern of transistors
the arithmetic that runs the show

reads the body's own circuitry
analogue to digital   each ECG translated
a ratio of binary numbers

Here the heart is all number
a lived graph of voltage and time
each heartbeat reckoned in sinus rhythm
or fluttering in chaotic arrhythmia

the heart in conflict with itself
logged   in a gold box recorder
the history of which is also a record of transit
from what countries or conflicts

the supply of gold   a chain
as fine as the minute wires of the chip
the flow of money that forces the heart
chambers that empty and fill with the flow of blood

that slips through borders   undetected

yet detectable   as a current
travelling the heart's conduction pathways

MARS DRILL BIT

> *designed to be assembled by autonomous robot*
> *to analyse the subsurface of Mars; tested in Antarctica*

Hollow core
to plumb a moon-struck planet
gone fishing in our own glassy archive

                      a column
drilled through ice rings   air bubbles'
frozen atmospheres   into the rock's
sub-glacial record
                  to hazard a guess
at past and future   sea levels   sunlight
and ice sheets   advancing, retreating

What path will it cut into the red planet's
fractured bedrock   cross-bedded
waves of sandstone   to reach
the gasses and isotopes
                  the cosmic oracles

    of that spinning, low-gravity spheroid
shovelled over by water and wind
                  a world
in which the alien
is a non-living explorer   sent out there
charged with the minds of its human creators
to assemble and disassemble
            the rig of our own strangeness

ENGINE

Model Newcomen steam engine
British (mid-18th century)

Wooden frame with cross pieces   metal cylinder
a piston attached by a chain and a pivoting beam
the cylinder open-topped
the frame open   light falls through it

From this machine
James Watt, *instrument maker*
(son of a trader in sugar and tobacco)
imagined a separate condenser
invented a future powered by steam

for iron mills
the cotton mills of the triangular trade
the sugar mills on the slave plantations
an engine driven by and driving
the boiling wheel of possession and dispossession

The object is marked with a red circle on a white roundel
the number '51' in red varnish

In this machine
(open, rectangular   light falling through it)
the past is prefigured
shackles   instruments of trauma
an iron collar attached to a chain
the chokeholds of the slave ships
the tally of lives that fuelled the future

VITRINE

Who stands beside me
under embossed pillars and clerestory windows
among labelled objects in a sheen of glass?

collected across oceans
bargained for with commonplace treasures
items listed once in a surgeon's journals
bills of sale or the guesswork of old inventories

hei tiki   beaded pouch   armlet of dog's teeth

gifts tied in a knot of meaning
loosed into the exchange of the saleroom
a disconnected array of sacred and profane
displayed to Europe's acquisitive gaze

Who sees   and who is seen?
Whose art has been framed as an object
akin to a bird's nest
a native architecture of twigs or rock?

Who is subject among the artefacts?

the Chinese jade of Miss Ina Smillie
ivory snow knife   sharkskin drum
Egyptian necklace and golden moons

a taiaha   wood, flax, feather, shell
collar winged   as a bird in flight

beyond the glass   is whirled
                    with the speed of a bird
                    a living presence

Who stands beside me
among simple or inexplicable instruments
on the high-lit gallery   a witness
to vanished gardens   the house
that once stood here   (residence
of Robert Bogle, West India Merchant)?

Is this the place
to take an angle on the past?
Quadrangles and pillared halls
built with the money of inheritors
their compensations   a wealth
that had seeped into this city like a sugar solution
a milk of amnesia

lustrous as the white glaze of the potteries
or the brass of *a telescope   (bequeathed*
by Alexander Macfarlane, plantation owner)

or *copper manillas*   (in the shape of bracelets
impossibly weighted for the wrists of babies)
currency or amulets
                    or slave tokens
                    each worth a human life

Can I   wanting the object in itself
however imperfectly understood
in the fact of its being

comprehend the living weight
of the unfinished   reverberant past
to which I am both witting and unwitting witness?

       Who am I   or another?

       Who is absent?   Who stands beside me?

              Who is my guide?

ACKNOWLEDGEMENTS

I blame it all on Alan Riach (friend, fellow poet and Professor of Scottish Literature at the University of Glasgow) whose projects to bring together poets and paintings and poets and museum objects first got me involved in the endlessly fascinating collection held by the Hunterian Museum. The provenance of museum objects is a complex area and whilst I have endeavoured to get the facts right, it is almost certain that I've slipped up somewhere. I would, however, like to thank Dr Andy Mills, Curator for Archaeology and World Cultures, and Dr Nicky Reeves, Curator for Scientific and Medical History Collections, for their best endeavours and for their generosity in responding to my queries. Amiria Henare's *Museums, Anthropology and Imperial Exchange* (CUP, 2005) was enlightening in relation to Maori artefacts and our understanding of the objects we encounter in museums. Warmest thanks go to Jane Routh, Mike Barlow, Carole Coates, Bill Gilson, Paul Mills and Ed Reiss for poems shared and discussed; and to Alan for reading the ms. Acknowledgements are due to the editors of *Imminent, Painted Spoken, Shearsman* and *Fras*, where some of these poems were first published. 'The Curiosities of Dr Hunter' was originally published in *The Hunterian Museum Poems*, edited by Alan Riach (The Hunterian & University of Glasgow, 2017).

NOTES TO THE POEMS

THE CURIOSITIES OF DR HUNTER focuses on objects which Hunter himself collected and which formed the original core of the Hunterian museum.

quartz in a chert concretion/one of Pococke's petrified melons: allegedly petrified melons, found in the Holy Land, and left over from the biblical flood. Richard Pococke was an eighteenth-century clergyman and travel-writer.

the anatomy of the human gravid uterus: Hunter's ground-breaking (1774) work on obstetrics with images of the foetus in utero, based on his dissection of pregnant bodies.

WITHOUT IMAGE

Most of the poems in this sequence engage with objects but this poem stems from my shock at coming across a human head, a tattooed preserved Maori head, in a display in the Hunterian Museum in the mid-eighties. Maori regard the remains of ancestors as tapu: to exhibit them or to see them exhibited in this way is a violation. The toi moko I saw then would have been one of four repatriated in 2009 to the guardianship of the Museum of New Zealand Te Papa Tongarewa. (Te Papa Tongarewa now uses the term toi moko for all preserved heads, though heads of slaves and captives produced for trade were originally known as mokomokai.) The Hunterian no longer holds toi moko in its collection.

WAKA HUIA

Treasure box. The word is formed from waka (canoe) and huia, the name of the wattlebird whose beautiful tail feathers were kept there. The huia became extinct in the early twentieth century after overhunting and loss of habitat.

WOODEN BOX WITH BRASS-HINGED LID

HMS Resolution was commanded by Captain Cook on his second voyage (1772–1775) during which he crisscrossed the Pacific and traversed the Antarctic circle, ruling out the existence of a Great Southern Continent.

ALTAR, SANDSTONE

found at Auchendavy Fort during the digging of the Forth and Clyde Canal in 1771.

CAST – by Jean-Baptiste Auguste Clésinger, 1849.

THREE HANDS

These particular wooden hands were probably designed to be displayed, perhaps for demonstration purposes, on the wooden plinth they are now on, rather than used.

GOLD STRUCK COIN WITH SHADOW

Setting out to write a poem about a Mary Queen of Scots gold ryal, I was delighted to discover the existence in the Hunterian collection of a fake ryal. See the student blog post by Cameron Maclean, Coin Room Volunteer at the Hunterian, 22 August 2019. http://hunterian.academicblogs.co.uk/2019/08/

AFTER-IMAGE

Emily Dix carried out pioneering work on the flora of the Upper Carboniferous and established a scheme of nine floral zones used to identify the succession of strata in the Coal Measures. Much of her research paperwork was destroyed in the World War II bombing of London. Her career was cut short by mental breakdown and lobotomy.

OPTICAL

Robert Hooke: English scientist and polymath, who in *Micrographia* (1665) first used the word cell to describe the honeycomb structure of cork which he likened to monks' cloisters.

animalcula: a term coined by seventeenth century Dutch scientist Antonie van Leeuwenhoek to describe microscopic organisms such as bacteria and protozoa.

LOG OF INTERMITTENT TRACINGS

Computer analysis of electrocardiograms was developed by the Electrocardiology Research Unit at the University of Glasgow from the 1960s onwards. The Pentium Pro processor unit was one of the most gold-rich computer chips ever made.

MARS DRILL BIT – developed by Dr Patrick Harkness and PhD students at the School of Engineering, University of Glasgow. Tested in Antarctica, the equipment performed so well that it was repurposed for scientific drilling of the bedrock below the ice sheets.

ENGINE

James Watt's father was a shipwright and merchant supplying the slave colonies of North America and the Caribbean and it was this which funded Watt's education. Watt retained an involvement in his father's business whilst working as an instrument-maker to the University of Glasgow. It was after his unsuccessful attempt to repair the university's model Newcomen steam engine that Watt came up with the solution of a separate condenser; this led eventually to Watt and Boulton's improved steam engine which hugely accelerated the pace of industrial development.

VITRINE

hei tiki: the carved pendant figure of Maori culture.

taiaha: a Maori fighting staff still used in a ceremonial challenge to visitors.

the money of inheritors: from 1866 to 1880 the University of Glasgow raised funds for a new campus at Gilmorehill, some of which undoubtedly came from people whose families had profited from slavery.

Alexander Macfarlane was a Scottish slave owner and planter based in Jamaica whose collection of astronomical instruments was bequeathed to the University of Glasgow. It was these instruments which James Watt was originally commissioned to restore.

copper manillas: manillas were used within West Africa as currency but European mass-produced manillas are associated with the Atlantic slave trade. After the ending of the slave trade they continued to be used locally and in the palm-oil trade. The date and provenance of the Hunterian's small number of manillas is uncertain.